I0448905

August 2013

WILDLAND FIRE MANAGEMENT

Improvements Needed in Information, Collaboration, and Planning to Enhance Federal Fire Aviation Program Success

GAO-13-684

GAO Highlights

Highlights of GAO-13-684, a report to congressional requesters

August 2013

WILDLAND FIRE MANAGEMENT

Improvements Needed in Information, Collaboration, and Planning to Enhance Federal Fire Aviation Program Success

Why GAO Did This Study

The Forest Service and Interior contract for aircraft to perform various firefighting functions, including airtankers that drop retardant. The Forest Service contracts for large airtankers and certain other aircraft, while Interior contracts for smaller airtankers and water scoopers. However, a decrease in the number of large airtankers, from 44 in 2002 to 8 in early 2013—due to aging planes and several fatal crashes—has led to concerns about the agencies' ability to provide aerial firefighting support.

GAO was asked to review agency efforts to ensure the adequacy of the firefighting aircraft fleet. This report examines (1) Forest Service and Interior efforts to identify the number and type of firefighting aircraft they need and (2) the Forest Service's approach to modernizing the large airtanker fleet and the challenges it faces in doing so. GAO reviewed agency studies and strategies, assessing the extent to which they included key elements important for understanding fire aviation needs; reviewed large airtanker planning and acquisition documents; and interviewed agency officials and representatives of the fire aviation community selected to represent state agencies, aircraft vendors, and others.

What GAO Recommends

GAO recommends, among other things, that the Forest Service and Interior expand efforts to collect information on the performance and effectiveness of firefighting aircraft and enhance collaboration across agencies and the fire aviation community. The agencies generally agreed with GAO's findings and recommendations.

View GAO-13-684. For more information, contact Anne-Marie Fennell at (202) 512-3841 or fennella@gao.gov.

What GAO Found

The Department of Agriculture's Forest Service and the Department of the Interior have undertaken nine major efforts since 1995 to identify the number and type of firefighting aircraft they need, but those efforts—consisting of major studies and strategy documents—have been hampered by limited information and collaboration. Specifically, the studies and strategy documents did not incorporate information on the performance and effectiveness of firefighting aircraft, primarily because neither agency collected such data. While government reports have long called for the Forest Service and Interior to collect aircraft performance information, neither agency did so until 2012 when the Forest Service began a data collection effort. However, the Forest Service has collected limited data on large airtankers and no other aircraft, and Interior has not initiated a data collection effort. In addition, although firefighting aircraft are often shared by federal agencies and can be deployed to support firefighting operations on federal and nonfederal lands, the agencies have not consistently collaborated with one another and other stakeholders to identify the firefighting aircraft they need. Many agency officials and stakeholders GAO contacted noted concerns about limited collaboration, and many cited shortcomings with the formal mechanism for collaboration—the National Interagency Aviation Committee. The committee has implemented some leading practices for collaboration such as defining and articulating a common purpose, but it has not taken additional steps to monitor and evaluate its collaborative activities, another leading practice. Collectively, additional information on aircraft performance and effectiveness and collaboration across agencies and with stakeholders could enhance agency estimates of their firefighting aircraft needs to more accurately represent national needs for such aircraft, and as a result, better position the agencies to develop strategic planning documents that represent those needs.

The Forest Service plans to modernize the large airtanker fleet by obtaining large airtankers from various sources over the near, medium, and long term, but each component of this approach faces challenges that make the continued availability of such aircraft to meet national fire suppression needs uncertain. In the near term, the agency plans to rely on a mix of contracted "legacy" airtankers as well as supplemental aircraft available through additional contracts and agreements with other governments and the military. However, agency concerns exist regarding the availability, capability, and costs of these resources. In the medium term, the Forest Service has awarded contracts for "next-generation" large airtankers that are faster and more up-to-date than most "legacy" aircraft, but it is uncertain when all of these aircraft will begin supporting fire suppression activities. Specifically, bid protests delayed contract issuance, and most of the aircraft receiving awards have not been fully tested and approved. In the long term, the Forest Service's plan includes purchasing certain large airtankers and obtaining others through intergovernmental transfer at no initial cost if they are declared surplus by the military—a shift from its long-standing practice of contracting for rather than owning aircraft. However, the Forest Service was unable to justify its previous plans for purchasing large airtankers to the Office of Management and Budget, and concerns exist regarding the retardant capacity and operating cost of the other airtankers it would obtain through intergovernmental transfer.

_____ United States Government Accountability Office

Contents

Figures

Abbreviations

CAL FIRE	California Department of Forestry and Fire Protection
DOD	Department of Defense
MAFFS	Modular Airborne Firefighting System
OMB	Office of Management and Budget

This is a work of the U.S. government and is not subject to copyright protection in the
United States. The published product may be reproduced and distributed in its entirety
without further permission from GAO. However, because this work may contain
copyrighted images or other material, permission from the copyright holder may be
necessary if you wish to reproduce this material separately.

GAO
U.S. GOVERNMENT ACCOUNTABILITY OFFICE

441 G St. N.W.
Washington, DC 20548

August 20, 2013

The Honorable Ron Wyden
Chairman
The Honorable Lisa Murkowski
Ranking Member
Committee on Energy and Natural Resources
United States Senate

The Honorable Dianne Feinstein
United States Senate

The Honorable Jon Tester
United States Senate

The Honorable Mark Udall
United States Senate

Over the last 5 decades, aircraft have played an important role in wildland fire suppression activities throughout the country by conducting aerial surveillance, delivering supplies and firefighters, and dropping retardant to slow fire growth or water to suppress fires. Federal, state, and local governments rely on firefighting aircraft—including fixed-wing airtankers, helicopters, and other aircraft—to help protect communities and natural resources from wildland fire, and experts project that, as fire seasons become longer and more severe, the need for firefighting aircraft will continue to grow. The federal government plays a central role in wildland fire response, including the use of firefighting aircraft, for which it largely relies on private vendors that own and operate the aircraft under contract to the government.

Among firefighting aircraft, large airtankers—those able to carry at least 1,800 gallons of fire retardant—are key resources for the federal government because they have the ability to fly to remote areas and quickly assist in containing small fires before they become larger, costlier, and more dangerous. However, the number of large airtankers available under federal contract decreased substantially in the last decade, from 44 in 2002 to 8 in early 2013.[1] The decrease of large airtankers in the federal

---

[1]Unless otherwise specified, all years cited in this report refer to calendar years.

GAO-13-684 Wildland Fire Management

fleet is, in part, the result of aircraft being retired due to their age—the average large airtanker is more than 50 years old—as well as agencies' concerns about the airtankers' safety and capability to perform a demanding fire aviation mission, which involves maneuvering aircraft at low speeds and altitude and enduring significant structural wing stress. Safety issues arose from two fatal crashes in 2002, both of which were caused by structural failures—specifically, wings separating from the aircraft during flight. These safety-related concerns led the government in 2011 to terminate contracts for eight large airtankers, which represented more than 40 percent of the federally-contracted large airtanker fleet at the time. Three additional crashes in 2012, two of which resulted in fatalities, further increased public concerns regarding the federal government's ability to provide continued aerial support for wildland firefighting activities.

Aircraft availability is also limited by the market characteristics for each type of aircraft. In particular, large airtankers are less available than other aircraft such as single-engine airtankers, helicopters, and surveillance aircraft.[2] Large airtankers have historically consisted of larger aircraft—typically surplus from the military—that were not designed to drop liquids and have undergone retrofitting to perform that mission. (See fig. 1 for examples of single-engine and large airtankers). According to the federal government's 2009 wildland fire aviation strategy, the availability of single-engine airtankers and helicopters is sufficient to meet national fire demands over the next 15 to 20 years, and the availability of aerial surveillance and smokejumper aircraft is adequate, but the Forest Service's recent large airtanker strategy notes that the economic difficulty for new vendors to enter the market or existing vendors to upgrade their fleets demonstrates the uncertainty regarding the continued availability of large airtankers.

---

[2]Single-engine airtankers are often agricultural aircraft designed to operate at low altitudes and configured to drop retardant rather than pesticides or fertilizer. Helicopters can perform multiple roles—including oil and gas, logging, and fire suppression support—and surveillance aircraft are typically general-purpose civilian aircraft.

Figure 1: Examples of Single-Engine and Large Airtankers Used in Wildland Fire Suppression

Sources: Air Tractor Inc. (left); GAO (right).

Air Tractor AT-802F single-engine airtanker.

Korean War-era Lockheed P-2V Neptune owned by Neptune Aviation Services, originally a maritime patrol aircraft now converted to a large airtanker.

Note: Large airtankers are defined by the agencies as aircraft with capacities of at least 1,800 gallons. Small, single-engine airtankers generally have capacities of 500 to 800 gallons.

The Department of Agriculture's Forest Service and the Department of the Interior's land management bureaus have a responsibility to respond to wildland fires on federal lands.[3] States and other entities—including tribal and local fire departments—have primary responsibility for responding to wildland fires on tribal, state, local, and private lands. Fighting wildland fires—which can burn across federal, state, and local jurisdictions—can require significant investments of personnel, aircraft, equipment, and supplies and can result in substantial fire suppression expenditures, with firefighting aircraft contributing to these costs. From 2007 through 2012, these agencies reported that more than $2.4 billion was spent on federally-contracted firefighting aircraft, fuel, and retardant.[4]

In light of questions about the availability of needed aerial support for firefighting—in particular the decrease in large airtanker availability—you

---

[3]The Department of the Interior includes four land management agencies: the Bureau of Indian Affairs, Bureau of Land Management, Fish and Wildlife Service, and National Park Service.

[4]This amount includes expenditures for both federal and nonfederal use of these contracted aircraft.

asked us to review federal agencies' efforts to ensure the adequacy of the federal firefighting aircraft fleet. This report examines (1) Forest Service and Interior efforts to identify the number and type of firefighting aircraft they need, and (2) the Forest Service's approach to modernizing the large airtanker fleet and the challenges it faces in doing so.

To examine Forest Service and Interior efforts to identify their firefighting aircraft needs, we identified and reviewed agency studies and strategy documents and interviewed agency officials responsible for managing fire aviation programs. We focused on those efforts conducted since 1995, when the Forest Service and Interior jointly conducted the first major study of their large airtanker needs. For each effort, we reviewed the methodologies used and identified the extent to which they included analysis of key elements, which we identified as important for understanding firefighting aircraft needs based on our reviews of multiple academic and agency studies and interviews with numerous stakeholders throughout the fire aviation community. The key elements we identified are: aircraft types, basing options, acquisition models, aircraft capabilities, suppression methods, and aircraft performance and effectiveness. We also interviewed agency officials about each effort to determine the extent of federal interagency collaboration involved. We compared the agencies' practices with GAO-identified leading practices for interagency collaboration.[5] To examine the Forest Service's approach to modernizing the large airtanker fleet and any challenges it faces in doing so, we reviewed agency documents related to large airtanker acquisition, management, and operations as well as planning and acquisition documents, such as the 2009 *Interagency Aviation Strategy*, the Forest Service's *2012 Large Airtanker Modernization Strategy*, and Forest Service airtanker contract solicitations, which lay out the agency's approach to obtaining large airtankers. For both objectives, we interviewed members of the fire aviation stakeholder community, including officials involved in the management and operations of aerial firefighting from the Forest Service, Interior and its four land management bureaus, the Department of Defense (DOD), and six state agencies that we selected based on input from federal agencies and the National Association of State Foresters; representatives from eight of the nine vendors we identified that own and operate large airtankers and that have

---

[5]See GAO, *Results-Oriented Government: Practices That Can Help Enhance and Sustain Collaboration among Federal Agencies*, GAO-06-15 (Washington, D.C.: Oct. 21, 2005).

responded to the most recent Forest Service contract solicitations;[6] and two national trade organizations, which we identified based on conversations with agency officials and vendor representatives. We also conducted site visits to the National Interagency Fire Center in Boise, Idaho;[7] the facilities of the only two private vendors with active Forest Service "legacy" large airtanker contracts, located in Minden, Nevada and Missoula, Montana; and the headquarters of California's fire aviation program—part of the California Department of Forestry and Fire Protection (CAL FIRE) in Sacramento.[8] The results of our interviews and site visits are not generalizable. Appendix I provides a more detailed description of our objectives, scope, and methodology.

We conducted this performance audit from August 2012 to August 2013 in accordance with generally accepted government auditing standards. Those standards require that we plan and perform the audit to obtain sufficient, appropriate evidence to provide a reasonable basis for our findings and conclusions based on our audit objectives. We believe that the evidence obtained provides a reasonable basis for our findings and conclusions based on our audit objectives.

Background

For decades, the federal government has relied on firefighting aircraft to assist in wildland fire suppression activities. These aircraft perform various firefighting activities, including gathering intelligence by detecting fires and conducting assessments of ongoing fires; delivering supplies such as water, food, and ground-based firefighting equipment; transporting firefighters; providing coordination and direction to aerial and ground-based firefighters; and delivering retardant or water to extinguish or slow the growth of fires. The federal government uses different types of firefighting aircraft, including large airtankers, very large airtankers, single-engine airtankers, amphibious fixed-wing water scoopers, helicopters, and fixed-wing surveillance and smokejumper aircraft to

---

[6]Representatives of the ninth vendor did not respond to our attempts to contact them.

[7]The National Interagency Fire Center is the nation's logistical support center for controlling and extinguishing wildland fires and coordinates the mobilization of fire suppression supplies, equipment, and personnel at the federal, regional, and local levels.

[8]CAL FIRE operates a fleet of airtankers, helicopters, and surveillance aircraft to assist in fire suppression activities. The federal government reimburses the state of California when these aircraft support fire suppression activities on federal lands.

perform these aerial fire suppression activities. Table 1 describes these firefighting aircraft and their functions. In general, multiple types of aircraft operate simultaneously to suppress fires. For example, airtankers that drop retardant or water often work in tandem with surveillance aircraft—lead planes—that coordinate the firefighting operation and guide the airtankers in dropping the retardant or water in the correct location. The 2013 *Interagency Standards for Fire and Fire Aviation Operations* defines several types of federal firefighting aircraft—including large and very large airtankers, large and medium helicopters, and surveillance and smokejumper aircraft—as national resources that can be deployed anywhere in the country and support fire suppression operations in any jurisdiction, including federal lands and nonfederal lands in accordance with relevant intergovernmental agreements.[9]

Table 1: Firefighting Aircraft Categories and Functions

Aircraft category	Aerial firefighting function(s)
Large and very large airtankers	Deliver a minimum of 1,800 gallons (for large airtankers) or 8,000 gallons (for very large airtankers) of retardant to help suppress wildland fires; their range allows for rapid deployment over long distances, enabling them to support fire suppression activities across geographic boundaries
Single-engine airtankers	Deliver smaller amounts of retardant—currently, up to 800 gallons—to help suppress wildland fires; due to their small size and aerodynamics, they are capable of great accuracy in rough terrain
Water scoopers	Deliver water collected from sources such as rivers or lakes for use in suppressing wildland fires; currently-contracted aircraft carry up to 1,400 gallons
Helicopters	Perform various firefighting functions, including transporting firefighters or supplies as well as delivering water or retardant
Surveillance aircraft	Provide command and control of aerial resources assigned to a fire as well as coordination and direction of ground forces engaged in fire suppression activities; one type—lead planes—guide airtankers over fires to assist in accurately targeting retardant delivery
Smokejumper aircraft	Deliver firefighters and supplies quickly to remote fires by parachute; the aircraft's mobility allows for rapid support on emerging fires

Source: GAO analysis of agency documents.

[9]Single-engine airtankers and small helicopters are not defined as national resources by the *Interagency Standards for Fire and Fire Aviation Operations*. Officials told us that such aircraft are limited in their range and speed, and as a result, they are generally deployed within a specific geographic area.

GAO-13-684 Wildland Fire Management

In most instances, firefighting aircraft that drop retardant or water do not extinguish wildland fires but instead slow the spread of fires or reduce their intensity as firefighters on the ground work to contain or suppress fires. Firefighting aircraft that deliver retardant or water support ground-based firefighters by performing two main functions: (1) dropping retardant around wildland fires to slow fire growth to provide ground-based firefighters additional time to build or reinforce fireline and (2) reducing the intensity of fires by dropping water directly on them.[10] In general, airtankers deliver retardant around fires to slow their spread, water scoopers drop water directly on fires to reduce their intensity, and helicopters can perform either function. Currently, all large and very large airtankers in the federal fleet are aircraft initially designed for other purposes—such as maritime patrol or civilian passenger transport—that have been retrofitted for the aerial fire suppression mission through the incorporation of retardant delivery systems—tanks affixed to aircraft that hold and release retardant.[11] Conversely, single-engine airtankers and water scoopers are built to drop retardant and water, respectively, to fight wildland fires.[12] Traditionally, airtankers have used retardant delivery systems that rely on gravity to evacuate retardant via doors that open in the bottom of the aircraft. However, some systems have been developed that use compressed air to force retardant out of the aircraft through nozzles rather than doors.

Fire suppression activities can generally be categorized as initial attack, extended attack, or large fire support. Initial attack activities include those conducted during the first "operational period" after the fire is reported, generally within 24 hours.[13] When fires are not controlled through initial attack, extended attack activities occur that generally involve the use of

---

[10]Fireline is an area where vegetation is cleared in an effort to stop the fire's spread at that point or slow it sufficiently to allow firefighters to attack directly. Firefighters often incorporate geographic features such as roads, rocky areas, or ridgelines into firelines to increase their effectiveness.

[11]In the United States, vendors have traditionally chosen retired military bombers, transport, and patrol aircraft to convert to large airtankers due to their availability and relatively low cost.

[12]Some water scoopers are also capable of dropping suppressant foam, which is applied directly on fires to reduce their intensity.

[13]An operational period is the period of time scheduled for execution of a given set of tactical actions. Operational periods can be of various lengths, although usually not more than 24 hours.

additional firefighting resources; when such fires grow large and complex, these activities may be referred to as large fire support. Federal and state wildland fire responders rely on a tiered interagency dispatch process for requesting and coordinating the use of firefighting resources, including aircraft, to respond to wildland fires. For example, when a wildland fire is reported, a local dispatch center identifies and dispatches, if available, fire response resources such as firefighters, aircraft, and equipment to perform initial attack activities. If sufficient resources are not available, local dispatch centers can request additional resources from the appropriate geographic area coordination center.[14] In the event that sufficient resources are not available within a geographic area, its geographic area coordination center can request additional resources from the National Interagency Coordination Center, which serves as the focal point for coordinating the mobilization of resources for wildland fire and other incidents throughout the United States.[15]

A number of interagency organizations develop interagency firefighting standards, including those pertaining to the development and use of firefighting aircraft, and coordinate federal firefighting efforts. To coordinate the overall firefighting efforts of the Forest Service and other federal land management agencies, the interagency National Wildfire Coordinating Group was established in 1974.[16] This interagency group develops and maintains standards, guidelines, and training and certification requirements for interagency wildland fire operations. Within this group, the National Interagency Aviation Committee is an interagency body of federal and state aviation operations managers responsible for providing common policy and direction for aviation resources involved in wildland firefighting.[17] This committee was established to serve as a body

---

[14]Eleven regional dispatch centers, called geographic area coordination centers, are located nationwide, each of which serves a specific geographic portion of the United States.

[15]The National Interagency Coordination Center is located at the National Interagency Fire Center in Boise, Idaho.

[16]The National Wildfire Coordinating Group draws on representatives from the Forest Service and from Interior's Bureau of Indian Affairs, Bureau of Land Management, Fish and Wildlife Service, and National Park Service, as well as the U.S. Fire Administration, National Association of State Foresters, and Intertribal Timber Council.

[17]Prior to April 2010, the National Interagency Aviation Committee was known as the National Interagency Aviation Council. We refer to the organization as the National Interagency Aviation Committee throughout this report.

of aviation experts, assisting the National Wildfire Coordinating Group with recognizing opportunities to enhance safety, effectiveness, and efficiency in aviation-related operations, procedures, programs, and coordination. In turn, the National Interagency Aviation Committee chartered the Interagency Airtanker Board to review and approve retardant and water delivery systems based on established performance criteria. The approval process—which includes an assessment of system design, testing of the systems' performance, and a physical inspection of the aircraft with system installed—ensures that the systems meet basic standards for delivery of retardant or water. Interagency Airtanker Board approval serves as a guide to participating federal and state agencies for identifying acceptable aircraft and retardant or water delivery systems that may compete for agency contracts.

The federal firefighting aircraft fleet includes some aircraft that are government owned, but most are obtained through contracts with private industry vendors. For example, the federal government owns some surveillance and smokejumper aircraft and contracts for the remainder, along with helicopters and aircraft that deliver retardant or water, from private industry vendors that own, operate, and maintain them. Currently, the Forest Service issues contracts for large and very large airtankers, as well as large and medium helicopters, and Interior issues contracts for single-engine airtankers and water scoopers.[18] The agencies use two types of contracts for obtaining firefighting aircraft from vendors: exclusive-use and call-when-needed.[19] Exclusive-use contracts require a vendor to provide an aircraft for service on any day covered by the "mandatory availability period" stipulated in the contract. The agencies pay vendors a daily rate regardless of whether the aircraft is used and also pay a fee for each hour flown if the aircraft is used. Conversely, call-when-needed contracts do not guarantee vendors any fee unless the aircraft is called upon to provide aerial fire support. This type of contract allows the government the flexibility to pay for firefighting aircraft only when they are used. However, the daily availability and flight hour rates for call-when-needed contracts are generally higher than those for

---

[18]Both agencies contract for small helicopters as well as smokejumper and surveillance aircraft.

[19]Forest Service uses the term "call-when-needed," and Interior uses the term "on-call" for contracts in which the agencies guarantee payment to the vendor contingent upon the aircraft being used. For the purposes of this report, we use the term call-when-needed to describe all such contracts.

exclusive-use contracts. In contrast to large airtankers, other types of firefighting aircraft are generally more available for federal contracting. For example, the agencies plan to have over 100 helicopters available in 2013 for fire suppression activities through exclusive-use contracts with hundreds more available through call-when-needed contracts. See appendix II for the number and types of aircraft in the federal firefighting aircraft fleet in 2013 and their associated cost rates.

The Forest Service and Interior have also established agreements with other governments (i.e., cooperator governments), as well as the military, to augment the national firefighting aircraft fleet during periods of heavy fire activity. The United States and Canada have established a mutual aid agreement whereby the National Interagency Coordination Center and the Canadian Interagency Forest Fire Centre can request firefighting resources, including aircraft, from each other during periods of heavy fire activity.[20] Similarly, some U.S. states and Canadian provinces have established regional intergovernmental agreements to facilitate the sharing of firefighting resources: the Northwest Fire Protection Agreement,[21] the Great Lakes Forest Fire Compact,[22] and the Northeastern Forest Fire Protection Compact.[23] Through these agreements, firefighting resources, including aircraft, can be dispatched from their contracted agency, state, or province to assist on fires on other lands covered by the agreement. The Forest Service can also obtain aerial firefighting support through the Modular Airborne Firefighting System (MAFFS) program under an agreement with DOD. Under this program, DOD provides Lockheed Martin C-130 Hercules aircraft as additional capacity for aerial firefighting when requested by the Forest Service. Each of the aircraft is equipped with a MAFFS unit—a portable,

---

[20]*Canada / United States Reciprocal Forest Fire Fighting Arrangement* (May 7, 1982). The arrangement is implemented in a series of annual operating plans, the most recent of which was issued on January 15, 2013.

[21]Signatories to the Northwest Fire Protection Agreement include the states of Alaska, Idaho, Montana, Oregon, and Washington, as well as the Canadian provinces of Alberta, British Columbia, and the Northwest and Yukon Territories.

[22]Members of the Great Lakes Forest Fire Compact include the states of Michigan, Minnesota, and Wisconsin, as well as the Canadian provinces of Manitoba and Ontario.

[23]Signatories to the Northeastern Forest Fire Protection Compact include the states of Connecticut, Maine, Massachusetts, New Hampshire, New York, Rhode Island, and Vermont, as well as the Canadian provinces of New Brunswick, Newfoundland and Labrador, Nova Scotia, and Quebec.

pressurized retardant delivery system that can be inserted into military C-130 aircraft to convert them into large airtankers when needed. The Forest Service owns the MAFFS units (eight in total) and provides the retardant, and DOD provides the C-130 aircraft, pilots, and maintenance and support personnel to fly the missions.[24] A new generation of MAFFS units became operational in February 2009, and the fleet has since transitioned to use this system exclusively.

Agencies' Efforts to Identify Firefighting Aircraft Needs Have Been Hampered by Limited Information and Collaboration

Since 1995, the Forest Service and Interior have cumulatively produced nine major studies and strategy documents related to their firefighting aviation needs, but the agencies' efforts to identify the number and type of firefighting aircraft needed have been hampered by limited information and collaboration. In particular, these efforts did not include information on the performance and effectiveness of firefighting aircraft and involved limited collaboration between agencies and with stakeholders in the fire aviation community.

Agency Efforts to Identify Firefighting Aircraft Needs Did Not Include Information on Performance and Effectiveness of Firefighting Aircraft

Forest Service and Interior efforts to identify the number and type of firefighting aircraft they need have largely consisted of developing major studies and strategy documents—nine since 1995. Based on reviews of academic and government studies and interviews with officials and representatives from across the fire aviation community, we identified the following key elements as important for understanding firefighting aircraft needs:

- Aircraft types – aircraft manufacturer, model, and size classification;
- Basing options – potential locations for aircraft bases;
- Acquisition models – options for obtaining aircraft, including purchasing aircraft or using vendor-owned aircraft;
- Aircraft capabilities – required capabilities of aircraft, such as retardant capacity and speed;
- Suppression methods – how to use aircraft to suppress fire, including initial attack and extended attack; and
- Aircraft performance and effectiveness – the results of using aircraft to support fire suppression activities.

---

[24]These aircraft are operated by Air National Guard units in California, North Carolina, and Wyoming, as well as an Air Force Reserve unit in Colorado.

While the Forest Service and Interior studies and strategy documents contained various key elements, none included information on performance and effectiveness of aircraft in helping to suppress wildland fires because agencies have not collected such information. Figure 2 identifies which key elements were included in each of the major studies and strategy documents we analyzed. (See app. III for additional information on each of these efforts.)

Figure 2: Key Elements Included in Major Forest Service and Interior Efforts Since 1995 to Identify Number and Type of Firefighting Aircraft They Need

Title of effort	Author(s)	Year	Aircraft types	Basing options	Acquisition models	Aircraft capabilities	Suppression methods	Aircraft performance and effectiveness
National Study of Airtankers to Support Initial Attack and Large Fire Suppression: Phase 1	Forest Service and Interior	1995	●	●				
National Study of (Large) Airtankers to Support Initial Attack and Large Fire Suppression: Phase 2	Forest Service and Interior	1996	●	●	●	●		
National Study of Tactical Aerial Resource Management to Support Initial Attack and Large Fire Suppression	Forest Service and Interior	1998	●	●	●	●	●	
Wildland Fire Management Aerial Application Study[a]	Fire Program Solutions, LLC[b]	2005	●	●	●	●	●	
Management Efficiency Assessment on Aviation Activities in the USDA Forest Service	Management Analysis, Incorporated[b]	2008	●	●				
National Interagency Aviation Council Interagency Aviation Strategy[c]	National Interagency Aviation Council	2009	●	●	●	●	●	
Forest Service Large Airtanker Modernization Strategy	Forest Service	2012	●			●	●	
Air Attack Against Wildfires: Understanding U.S. Forest Service Requirements for Large Aircraft	Rand Corporation[b]	2012	●					
Firefighting Aircraft Study	Avid LLC[b]	2013		●				

Source: GAO analysis of agency efforts.

Note: Other studies of firefighting aviation have been published but are not included here because they did not include efforts to identify the appropriate number or type of firefighting aircraft. See, for example, Blue R bbon Panel, Federal Aerial Firefighting: Assessing Safety and Effectiveness (December 2002).

[a]The 2005 Wildland Fire Management Aerial Application Study is the third phase of the National Study of Airtankers to Support Initial Attack and Large Fire Suppression.

[b]The Forest Service contracted a private company to conduct this study.

[c]As previously noted, the National Interagency Aviation Council became known as the National Interagency Aviation Committee in April 2010. The Forest Service, Interior, Bureau of Indian Affairs, Bureau of Land Management, Fish and Wildlife Service, National Park Service, and National Association of State Foresters participate in the National Interagency Aviation Committee and assisted in developing this strategy.

The agencies generally used cost- and efficiency-based metrics in these efforts, such as the potential cost of damage from wildland fires or the frequency with which requests for firefighting aircraft are unmet, to identify their firefighting aircraft needs. For example, the three-part *National Study of Airtankers to Support Initial Attack and Large Fire Suppression*, conducted from 1995 to 2005, estimated the number of large airtankers needed by comparing the cost of using large airtankers to help suppress wildland fires with the projected cost of the damage that could result from not suppressing the fires. In addition, the Forest Service's 2013 *Firefighting Aircraft Study* focused on efficiency and identified the number of large airtankers needed by analyzing the annual number of requests for these aircraft that the Forest Service was unable to meet.[25] However, agency efforts to identify their firefighting aircraft needs have not included information on the performance and effectiveness of using aircraft to suppress wildfires primarily because neither the Forest Service nor Interior has collected data on these aspects of firefighting aircraft. Specifically, the agencies have not established data collection mechanisms to track the specific tactical uses of firefighting aircraft—for example, where retardant or water is dropped in relation to a fire as well as the objective of a drop, such as protecting a structure or preventing a fire from moving in a specific direction—or measure their performance and effectiveness in those uses. Moreover, a 2012 study by the Forest Service's Rocky Mountain Research Station found that the Forest Service did not collect information about the locations where airtankers drop retardant or the actual performance and effectiveness of these aircraft.[26]

[25]Specifically, this study analyzed requests submitted by incident commanders or other firefighting officials seeking firefighting aircraft support on individual fires. Such requests are entered into an agency resource ordering system, which tracks the number of filled and unfilled requests. The study also analyzed the number of unfilled requests for large helicopters, but it did not identify the number of large helicopters needed.

[26]Matthew P. Thompson, David E. Calkin, Jason Herynk, Charles W. McHugh, and Karen C. Short, "Airtankers and Wildfire Management in the US Forest Service: Examining Data Availability and Exploring Usage and Cost Trends," *International Journal of Wildland Fire* (August 2012).

In May 2012, we reported on the importance of performance information in another context and found that such information can inform key management decisions, such as allocating resources, or it can help determine progress in meeting the goals of programs or operations.[27]

General agreement exists among wildland firefighters that, based on their experience, using aircraft can be beneficial to suppressing fires, but little empirical data exist to measure the performance and effectiveness of such aircraft use. For example, a 2007 study cited anecdotal evidence that firefighting aircraft saved homes, and a 2012 study that surveyed fire management officials found that these officials believed aircraft were effective in reducing the amount of time required to contain wildfires, particularly in the most difficult fire suppression conditions.[28] However, such views are not based on empirical data on aircraft performance and effectiveness, and other studies—including the Forest Service's 2013 *Firefighting Aircraft Study*—found that no accurate information on the effectiveness of aerial fire suppression exists and noted that the factors contributing to the success of wildfire suppression efforts are poorly understood.[29] Further, the 2009 *Interagency Aviation Strategy* stated it is difficult to assess the relative value of delivering retardant or water through helicopters, large airtankers, and single-engine airtankers and called for analytic tools focusing on this area to be developed. In addition, the 1998 *National Study of Tactical Aerial Resource Management* identified the need for better information on the intended use of surveillance aircraft—such as support for initial attack or large fire suppression activities—to determine the specific types of aircraft that will meet federal needs for aerial surveillance during firefighting.

---

[27]GAO, *Nanotechnology: Improved Performance Information Needed for Environmental, Health, and Safety Research,* GAO-12-427 (Washington, D.C.: May 21, 2012).

[28]See M. Plucinski, J. Gould, G. McCarthy, and J. Hollis, "The Effectiveness and Efficiency of Aerial Firefighting in Australia, Part 1," Bushfire Cooperative Research Centre, Technical Report A0701 (June 2007), and M. Plucinski, J. McCarthy, J. Hollis, and J. Gould, "The Effect of Aerial Suppression on the Containment Time of Australian Wildfires Estimated by Fire Management Personnel," *International Journal of Wildland Fire* 21 (December 2011): 219-229.

[29]See, for example, Avid, LLC, "Firefighting Aircraft Study," AG-024B-C-12-0006 (Yorktown, VA: Feb. 27, 2013) and Mark A. Finney, Isaac C. Grenfell, and Charles W. McHugh, "Modeling Containment of Large Wildfires Using Generalized Linear Mixed-Model Analysis," *Forest Science*, 55, no. 3, (June 2009): 249-255.

This limited availability of information on the performance and effectiveness of firefighting aircraft is an area of long-standing concern; since the 1960s, multiple reviews of federal fire aviation programs have called for the Forest Service and Interior to collect information on the performance of firefighting aircraft but neither agency has taken action until recently.[30] Specifically, in May 2012, the Forest Service recognized the need for an approach to evaluate the effective and efficient use of firefighting aircraft and began a project on aerial firefighting use and effectiveness to develop technology, evaluation criteria, and performance measures to quantify and assess the effective use of large airtankers, helicopters, and water scoopers in delivering retardant, water, and fire-suppressing chemicals.[31] According to Forest Service documents, the agency plans to collect information including whether an aircraft was used for initial attack or extended attack; the aircraft's objective, such as building a line of retardant, directly suppressing fire, or protecting a specific structure; whether the fire is in grass, shrub, or timber; general weather conditions; and characteristics of the actual drop of retardant, such as the time, aircraft speed, retardant amount, and outcome.[32] The agency collected some of this information during 2012, but it has not developed incremental goals for assessing progress or timelines for completing the project.

The Forest Service faces several challenges in carrying out its project on aerial firefighting use and effectiveness. For example, during 2012, the agency collected information on the performance and effectiveness of one type of aircraft—large airtankers—from about 25 fires but needs information on several hundred fires to perform useful analysis on large airtanker performance, according to Forest Service officials managing the data collection effort. These officials said that it will likely take several years for the agency to collect the information needed to analyze and

---

[30]See, for example, Forest Service, *Airtanker Retardant Drop Evaluation Study*, 1964, and Department of Agriculture Office of Inspector General, *Audit Report: Forest Service's Replacement Plan for Firefighting Aerial Resources*, 08601-53-SF (Washington, D.C.: July 16, 2009).

[31]The working title of this project is the *Aerial Firefighting Use and Effectiveness Study*.

[32]The Forest Service plans to collect this information by using existing processes, such as gathering reports from aerial firefighters who observe aircraft dropping retardant or water to suppress fires. Forest Service officials told us that the agency also uses non-traditional processes to collect information, such as infrared imagery, ground photos, and aircraft tracking sensors.

understand the effectiveness of the three types of firefighting aircraft—large airtankers, helicopters, and water scoopers—included in the project. Forest Service officials also told us that aerial firefighters have been reluctant to collect information on the results of using firefighting aircraft for several reasons, including safety concerns regarding adding to the workload of aerial firefighters while they are flying over fires, firefighters' concerns that Forest Service will use the information to criticize their performance, a firefighting culture that values experience and history over data and scientific analysis, and the challenges in finding time to complete data collection while fighting wildfires. Interior officials said that the department is assisting the Forest Service in this data collection project but does not currently have plans to collect performance information on the firefighting aircraft it manages.

Large airtankers have been the focus of the Forest Service's current data collection effort as well as the agencies' prior studies and strategy documents, but few efforts have focused on other types of firefighting aircraft. Specifically, eight of the agencies' nine studies and strategy documents attempted to identify the appropriate number of large airtankers for the federal fleet. However, only three of the efforts—the 1998 *National Study of Tactical Aerial Resource Management*, the 2009 *Interagency Aviation Strategy*, and the 2012 *Air Attack Against Wildfires: Understanding U.S. Forest Service Requirements for Large Aircraft*—identified the number of other types of aircraft needed,[33] despite the fact that each type of firefighting aircraft provides unique capabilities to support fire suppression operations. For example, water scoopers can deliver large quantities of water when a fire ignites near a water source, smokejumper aircraft can quickly transport firefighters and supplies to fires in remote areas, and helicopters have the versatility to transport firefighters, supplies, or small quantities of water or retardant. As a result, performance and effectiveness information on all types of firefighting aircraft helps agencies identify the number and type of firefighting aircraft they need, including assessing any potential new firefighting aircraft platforms or technologies that vendors may propose; understand the strengths and limitations of each type of aircraft in different situations; and understand how firefighting aircraft could help achieve their wildfire

---

[33]The 1998 study recommended the appropriate number of surveillance aircraft, the 2009 study recommended the appropriate number for all aircraft types, and the 2012 study recommended the appropriate number of large airtankers, large helicopters, and water scoopers.

suppression goals. Obtaining information about aircraft performance and effectiveness could better inform agency estimates of firefighting aircraft needs to include in their strategies for obtaining aircraft, thus helping agencies better ensure the adequacy of the federal firefighting aircraft fleet.

In contrast to U.S. federal agencies, some foreign and U.S. state governments that operate aerial firefighting programs have employed various methods to collect and use performance and effectiveness information on their firefighting aircraft.[34] For example, in Canada, the British Columbia Forest Service requires aerial firefighters to complete an airtanker data report immediately after each airtanker flight. Officials then compile information gathered through these reports with information from their dispatch system to evaluate airtanker performance using a set of key performance indicators, such as the amount of time from the initial report of a fire to the time that an airtanker request is entered into the dispatch system, the distance between available airtankers and the actual fire, and the change in the size of the fire from the time an aircraft arrives at the fire to the time the fire is contained. According to British Columbia Forest Service officials, the performance information and indicators have been integral to improving British Columbia's aerial firefighting program. For example, officials found that available aircraft were often over 100 miles from the wildfires where they dropped retardant. Based on this analysis, the province made significant changes to its methods for pre-positioning firefighting aircraft and as a result, available aircraft are generally within 60 miles of a wildfire. In addition, the Minnesota Department of Natural Resources requires officials to complete debriefing reports after each use of firefighting aircraft. The report includes information on the specific aircraft that were sent to the fire and gathers the firefighters' views on whether areas such as dispatch information, aircraft briefings, target descriptions, and communications were adequate or need improvement. According to Minnesota Department of Natural Resources officials,

---

[34]In the United States, numerous state governments operate aerial firefighting programs of varying sizes that use numerous types of aircraft. Of the state officials we met with—representing Alaska, California, Florida, Minnesota, New Hampshire, and Texas—Minnesota state government officials reported collecting aircraft performance information. While several foreign governments—including Australia, multiple Canadian provinces, France, and Italy—operate aerial firefighting programs, we spoke to British Columbia province officials because the Forest Service identified British Columbia's collection and use of airtanker performance information as a leading practice.

information from these reports may help determine the best methods for suppressing fires when a specific set of aircraft is available.

Agencies Have Not Consistently Collaborated with One Another or with Other Stakeholders to Identify Firefighting Aircraft Needs

In efforts to identify the number and type of firefighting aircraft they need, agencies have engaged in limited collaboration with one another or with other stakeholders in the fire aviation community. For example, the Forest Service developed its 2012 *Large Airtanker Modernization Strategy* without obtaining input from representatives of state fire aviation programs or the large airtanker industry and did not coordinate with Interior until after the development of an initial draft. According to several agency officials we spoke with, the Forest Service did not invite Interior officials to provide their input on the strategy until after the agency sent the draft version to the Office of Management and Budget (OMB) for review and approval. Similarly, regarding Interior, senior Interior officials told us that Interior generally does not involve other agencies or stakeholders in developing annual estimates of the number of each type of aircraft to obtain through contracts. Rather, Interior develops these estimates by asking relevant Interior bureaus to provide the number of each type of aircraft it needs, compiling these estimates, and adjusting them based on available funding.

The importance of collaboration with stakeholders and agencies has been noted in several government reports.[35] For example, the interagency 2009 *Quadrennial Fire Review* identified the need to engage agency leaders, partners, and industry in a strategic dialogue about the demands for firefighting resources, such as aircraft, and noted the importance of innovative and efficient ways to meet those demands.[36] Additionally, a 2009 Department of Agriculture Inspector General's report recommended that the Forest Service collaborate with stakeholders in the fire aviation

---

[35]The importance of collaboration was noted in a 2002 report by an expert panel that Forest Service and Interior convened to examine the safety and effectiveness of federal aerial firefighting. This report identified collaboration among agencies, contractors, and states as possibly the single largest aerial firefighting challenge facing federal agencies at the time. See Blue Ribbon Panel, *Federal Aerial Firefighting: Assessing Safety and Effectiveness* (December 2002).

[36]The Quadrennial Fire Review is a strategic assessment process that is conducted every 4 years to evaluate current mission strategies and capabilities against best estimates of the future environment for wildfire management. This integrated review is a joint effort of the five federal natural resource management agencies and their state, local, and tribal partners that constitute the wildland fire community.

community to develop goals and performance measures for the agency's aviation strategic plan.[37] Regarding collaboration with stakeholders, in April 2013, we reported that when agencies carry out activities in a fragmented and uncoordinated way, the resulting patchwork of programs can waste scarce funds, confuse and frustrate program customers, and limit the overall effectiveness of the federal effort.[38] In addition, we reported in October 2011 that successful organizations involve stakeholders in developing their mission, goals, and strategies to help ensure that they target the highest priorities.[39] In that report, we also stated that stakeholders can influence success or failure of agencies' programs.

Many Forest Service and Interior officials, as well as other stakeholders, we spoke with expressed concerns about limited collaboration, and many cited shortcomings with the formal mechanism for interagency collaboration—the National Interagency Aviation Committee, which includes representatives from the Forest Service, Interior and its bureaus, and the National Association of State Foresters. Some stakeholders told us the committee has not always considered the needs of all agencies involved in firefighting efforts. For example, in 2008 committee members collaboratively developed a national firefighting aviation strategy, the *Interagency Aviation Strategy*. A year later, however, the Forest Service developed an appendix to the strategy that outlined the Forest Service's plans for replacing its large airtanker fleet, and the committee published an amended strategy—including that appendix—without providing member agencies the opportunity to review or contribute to it, according to agency officials. As a result, the large airtanker appendix does not reflect the opinions of all committee members, and consequently does not reflect the needs of the fire aviation community stakeholders that will require the use of large airtankers. In addition, Forest Service and Interior officials told us that agency staff who serve on the committee are generally firefighting operations staff and do not represent senior agency

---

[37]Department of Agriculture Office of Inspector General, *Audit Report: Forest Service's Replacement Plan for Firefighting Aerial Resources* (Washington, D.C.: July 16, 2009).

[38]GAO, *2013 Annual Report: Actions Needed to Reduce Fragmentation, Overlap, and Duplication and Achieve Other Financial Benefits*, GAO-13-279SP (Washington, D.C.: Apr. 9, 2013).

[39]GAO, *Environmental Justice: EPA Needs to Take Additional Actions to Help Ensure Effective Implementation*, GAO-12-77 (Washington, D.C.: Oct. 6, 2011).

management. As a result, the collaboration that occurs through the committee is often limited to day-to-day operations activities rather than broader strategic efforts.

The committee has implemented some leading practices that we previously reported can help enhance and sustain collaboration.[40] Specifically, the committee's members have defined and articulated a common purpose and have agreed on agency roles and responsibilities. For example, the committee's charter identifies its purpose as serving as a body of aviation experts focused on identifying opportunities to enhance safety, effectiveness, and efficiency in aviation related operations, procedures, programs, and coordination. In addition, the committee's 2009 *Interagency Aviation Strategy* defines the general aerial firefighting roles and responsibilities of federal and state agencies as well as aircraft contracting responsibilities of the Forest Service and Interior. However, we previously found that agencies often face a range of barriers, including concerns about controlling jurisdiction over missions and resources, when they attempt to collaborate with other agencies.[41] Interior officials told us that the division of firefighting aircraft contracting responsibilities among the Forest Service and Interior—under which Forest Service issues contracts for large and very large airtankers and large and medium helicopters, while Interior issues contracts for single-engine airtankers and water scoopers—may not foster a culture of collaboration since each agency is focused on its own aircraft of responsibility. Although the committee has implemented some leading practices for collaboration, it has not taken additional steps to reinforce agency accountability for collaboration, such as developing mechanisms to monitor, evaluate, and report the results of collaborative efforts.[42] We have reported that by creating the means to monitor, evaluate, and report the results of their collaborative efforts, federal agencies can better identify areas for improvement, although the specific ways in which this practice is implemented may differ based on the specific collaboration challenges agencies face. For example, mechanisms for monitoring the results of collaborative efforts may range from occasional meetings among agency officials to more formal periodic reviews where officials from each agency

---

[40]GAO-06-15.

[41]GAO, *Managing for Results: Barriers to Interagency Coordination*, GAO/GGD-00-106 (Washington, D.C.: Mar. 29, 2000).

[42]GAO-06-15.

report on progress toward achieving the goals of interagency collaborative efforts. As we reported in August 2012, absent effective collaboration, interagency efforts could result in limited information being communicated and opportunities for incorporating stakeholder input being missed.[43]

Senior management in both the Forest Service and Interior told us they have begun discussions regarding how to improve their interagency collaboration. However, they said that these discussions have focused on obtaining firefighting aircraft for the 2013 fire season and have not yet addressed collaboration on strategic planning issues. Further, both Forest Service and Interior officials told us the *Interagency Aviation Strategy* is outdated and should be updated to more accurately reflect current firefighting aircraft needs. Engaging in effective collaboration to incorporate input from all fire aviation community stakeholders could better position the agencies in developing strategic planning documents— including any updates to the *Interagency Aviation Strategy*—that represent the national need for firefighting aircraft.

The Forest Service's Approach to Modernizing the Large Airtanker Fleet Faces Challenges, Resulting in Uncertainty over Continued Large Airtanker Availability

The Forest Service plans to modernize the large airtanker fleet by obtaining large airtankers from various sources over the near, medium, and long terms, but each component of this approach faces challenges that make the continued availability of such aircraft to meet national fire suppression needs uncertain. The components of the agency's approach include: (1) in the near term, continuing to contract with private vendors for "legacy" large airtankers—generally aging aircraft with limited future service life spans—on exclusive-use contracts and very large airtankers on call-when-needed contracts, as well as relying on agreements with cooperator governments and the military; (2) in the medium term, contracting with vendors for airtankers that are more modern and capable than those generally in use currently; and (3) in the long term, acquiring new federally-owned aircraft with expected service life spans of up to 30 years. Additionally, some federal and state agencies are considering alternative plans to obtaining aerial fire suppression support to reduce reliance on large airtankers.

---

[43]GAO, *Housing Assistance: Opportunities Exist to Increase Collaboration and Consider Consolidation*, GAO-12-554 (Washington, D.C.: Aug. 16, 2012).

The Forest Service's Near-term Approach Includes Using "Legacy" and Supplemental Airtankers but Concerns Exists Regarding Aircraft Availability, Performance, or Cost	For the near-term, the Forest Service plans to primarily rely on exclusive-use "legacy" contracts to obtain large airtankers. However, during periods of heavy fire activity, the agency plans to obtain supplemental airtankers through call-when-needed contracts for very large airtankers, agreements with cooperator governments, and military aircraft equipped with MAFFS. However, agency officials and vendor representatives told us about limitations and challenges—including availability, performance, and cost—regarding these resources.
"Legacy" Large Airtankers	Over the next 5 years—including the 2013 fire season—the Forest Service plans to rely on aircraft obtained through its "legacy" exclusive-use contracts, which has been the agency's traditional acquisition model for obtaining large airtankers. The agency in 2013 announced contract awards for nine aircraft: seven P-2V Neptunes—Korean War-era piston-engine maritime patrol aircraft—and two British Aerospace BAe-146s—converted versions of modern commercial jets.[44] However, the availability of the P-2V Neptunes in the short term is uncertain, and the Interagency Airtanker Board has documented concerns regarding performance of the retardant delivery systems on these BAe-146s.

- *Lockheed P-2V Neptune.* The age of the seven P-2V Neptunes—they average more than 50 years old—makes their availability throughout the entire 5-year contract period uncertain. Specifically, vendors told us they might need to retire some aircraft prior to the end of the current contract period because of the cost of maintaining the aging aircraft. In particular, they told us that the limited availability of replacement parts—and the difficulty of manufacturing new ones if no others exist—coupled with the requirements of increased maintenance and inspection standards make the P-2V Neptune difficult to operate in a cost-effective manner. Further, physical stresses on the aircraft could cause cracking of critical components during fire missions. For example, representatives from Neptune Aviation Services told us that the vendor retired one of its P-2V

---

[44]These contracts were awarded to two vendors: Neptune Aviation Services (six P-2V Neptunes and two BAe-146s) and Minden Air Corp (one P-2V Neptune). The Forest Service initially awarded a contract for a single BAe-146, but added another based on concerns regarding the overall availability of large airtankers for the 2013 fire season. The P-2V Neptunes are capable of delivering approximately 2,000 gallons of retardant and the BAe-146s approximately 2,600 gallons.

GAO-13-684 Wildland Fire Management

Neptunes after the 2012 fire season due to structural problems discovered during routine maintenance.[45] They also said that the vendor probably could continue to operate approximately five P-2V Neptunes for the next 10 years but that the current heavy use of their fleet could shorten this timeframe. Ultimately, Neptune Aviation Services plans to retire its P-2V Neptune fleet and transition to operating modern aircraft exclusively.

- *Neptune Aviation Services' British Aerospace BAe-146s.* Concerns regarding the performance of the retardant delivery system on Neptune Aviation Services' BAe-146s have been documented during agency evaluations of the aircraft and were voiced by several agency officials we interviewed.[46] During initial assessment of the system in 2011, the Interagency Airtanker Board determined that the retardant delivery system did not meet established performance criteria and identified problems regarding the system's design and performance.[47] However, in September 2012, the board approved, on an interim basis, the use of the retardant delivery system through the 2012 fire season so that information on its operational effectiveness could be collected and design deficiencies addressed. During the 2012 fire season, the BAe-146s collectively made approximately 300 retardant drops, which the board considered sufficient to collect data needed to assess their operational effectiveness.

In December 2012, the Interagency Airtanker Board declined to extend the interim approval of Neptune Aviation Services' BAe-146 system, citing the problematic retardant delivery system design and deficient performance during the 2012 fire season. In February 2013, however, the National Interagency Aviation Committee determined that the need for aircraft to deliver retardant for the 2013 fire season was sufficiently important to override the board's decision. As a result,

---

[45]Representatives of Minden Air Corp told us that the company no longer operates one of its two P-2V Neptunes following damaged sustained from a controlled-crash landing caused by landing gear failure during the 2012 fire season.

[46]The retardant delivery system of this specific BAe-146 differs from traditional systems; it uses a series of tubes to evacuate retardant from the aircraft rather than doors.

[47]Specifically, this initial assessment determined that the system did not have the range of variability of retardant flow rates normally found in proposed systems, the consistency of retardant flow trailed off as the retardant tank emptied, and the system was unable to predictably drop retardant while in a nose-down descent—a common flight profile for dropping retardant downhill.

the board, at the direction of the committee, granted an extension of its interim approval of the retardant delivery system through December 15, 2013. Representatives of Neptune Aviation Services acknowledged that the system has limitations, but they stated that the company is developing a revised retardant delivery system and plans to retrofit all of its BAe-146 aircraft with the updated design by the beginning of the 2014 fire season. However, the Interagency Airtanker Board has noted that the deficiencies may persist due to the inherent design of the system, and fire management officials from the Forest Service, Interior, and several states that are familiar with this aircraft told us they have reservations about the retardant delivery system's performance.

Very Large Airtankers

The Forest Service announced call-when-needed contracts for two very large airtankers—converted versions of Boeing 747 and McDonnell Douglas DC-10 commercial jets—to provide extended attack and large fire support beginning in 2013 with durations of up to 3 years. However, some agency officials cited concerns about the aircrafts' role, suitability for operating over rugged terrain, limited compatibility with current airtanker base infrastructure, and high costs (see fig. 3 for an example of a very large airtanker).[48]

---

[48]Two vendors developed very large airtankers during the early 2000s, with each retrofitting a different type of aircraft—10 Tanker Air Carrier converted two McDonnell Douglas DC-10s with retardant capacities of 11,600 gallons, and Evergreen International Aviation converted a Boeing 747 with a retardant capacity of 19,400 gallons.

Figure 3: Example of a DC-10 Very Large Airtanker Dropping Retardant

Source: 10 Tanker Air Carrier.

The Forest Service previously contracted for very large airtankers, but according to Forest Service and Interior officials, firefighters were initially reluctant to request the very large airtankers for several reasons. For example, because of the size of these aircraft, some federal officials were uncertain whether they could safely operate in rugged terrain.[49] Some officials also told us that firefighters did not request very large airtankers because they were uncertain how best to use this new tool. For example, the Forest Service identifies the primary mission of large airtankers as initial attack, whereas the solicitation for the very large airtanker call-when-needed contract stated that they will be used to provide support for

---

[49]To evaluate the safety and utility of very large airtankers, in 2009 the Forest Service contracted with the National Aeronautics and Space Administration to conduct an operational test and evaluation of both types of very large airtanker. This evaluation concluded that the aircraft could probably operate with few restrictions over gently rolling terrain but that extra restrictions might be necessary in extremely steep or rugged terrain. *USFS Very Large Aerial Tanker Operational Test and Evaluation Summary Report*, March 2, 2009. Representatives from 10 Tanker Air Carrier, which operates the DC-10s, told us that their aircraft have successfully delivered retardant in rugged terrain since 2006.

extended attack on large fires—leading to uncertainty about the best tactics for employing them.[50] Despite early reluctance to use very large airtankers, officials noted increased reliance on these aircraft; nevertheless, some agency officials continue to disagree about the most effective role—initial attack or large fire support—for these aircraft as well as whether or not they are suited to operating above rugged terrain. Additionally, very large airtankers can operate out of a limited number of established airtanker bases because their weight and size are too great for some existing base infrastructure such as runways or aircraft parking areas. Specifically, about half of the large airtanker bases nationwide—35 of 67—are currently or potentially capable of supporting DC-10 operations, according to a Forest Service official;[51] the 747's compatibility with bases is even more limited in that it can operate from approximately 12 locations, not all of which are airtanker bases. However, some agency officials told us that the speed of these aircraft can compensate for their limited compatibility with existing airtanker bases and associated increased distances that the aircraft might need to fly to respond to fires. Some officials also noted concerns about the high costs of using the aircraft. (See app. II for the current contract rates of firefighting aircraft.)

Cooperator Government Airtankers

The Forest Service plans to request large airtankers from two cooperator governments—Canada and the State of Alaska—during periods of high fire activity but these aircraft may not always be available. Under an agreement originally established in 1982, the Forest Service plans to rely on five Convair CV-580 large airtankers—converted commercial aircraft with retardant capacities of 2,100 gallons—provided by Canadian provinces as additional resources when additional large airtankers are needed. Additionally, Forest Service officials told us that, under a separate agreement, the agency can also request use of three CV-580s contracted by the State of Alaska. However, the use of these airtankers to supplement the federal large airtanker fleet is contingent upon the cooperator governments making them available. For example, such airtankers might already be committed to suppressing fires, which could prevent them from being released to assist other governments.

---

[50]Both very large airtanker vendors told us that their aircraft are capable of supporting initial attack operations.

[51]The potential ability of 21 airtanker bases to support DC-10 operations may be contingent upon the availability of mobile retardant loading equipment.

Modular Airborne Firefighting System (MAFFS)

As it has periodically done since the program's inception in the early 1970s, the Forest Service plans to rely on the military to provide surge aerial firefighting capacity through the deployment of up to eight MAFFS-equipped C-130 aircraft (see fig. 4 for an example of a MAFFS-equipped C-130).[52] However, a number of officials from the Forest Service, Interior, and state fire agencies stated that MAFFS performance can be inadequate in some circumstances. For example, while a Forest Service official noted that the MAFFS system has been approved by the Interagency Airtanker Board, some federal and state fire aviation officials told us that the retardant line dispersed by the MAFFS system is generally narrower than firefighters prefer, which can either allow a fire to jump across the retardant line or necessitate an additional drop to widen the line, if another aircraft is available. Additionally, some officials said the system is unable to penetrate dense forest canopies, thereby preventing the retardant from being effective when used in heavy timber. However, some federal and state officials told us that MAFFS can be used effectively on rangeland where grasses are the predominant fuel type.

Further, some fire officials expressed concern regarding the limited experience that MAFFS crews may have in the fire aviation mission because they are not full-time aerial firefighters. A DOD accident investigation report conducted in response to a 2012 fatal crash of a MAFFS-equipped C-130H found that the limited total firefighting experience of the crew—in particular, the number of drops accomplished prior to the accident—was a contributing factor to the accident.[53] The report also stated that the crew's training did not include essential components—including training on local terrain conditions and congested airtanker base operations—necessary to conduct MAFFS operations in the region where the crash occurred. A Forest Service official involved in managing MAFFS training told us that the agency has updated the training to better incorporate such components.

---

[52]The Forest Service is responsible, through the National Interagency Fire Center, for reimbursing DOD for the actual costs of MAFFS activation. DOD estimates the per-hour flight costs of MAFFS to be between about $4,700 and $8,000 dollars depending on the model of C-130 used, with variable daily availability costs depending on factors including the number of personnel required as well as the location of the activation. A Forest Service budget official told us that the combined reimbursements to DOD for MAFFS training and operational use from 2007 to 2012 totaled nearly $87 million.

[53]*United States Air Force Accident Investigation Board Report C-130H3, T/N 93-1458* (Oct. 27, 2012).

Figure 4: Example of MAFFS-equipped C-130

Source: U.S. Air Force.

Note: This figure depicts a MAFFS-equipped C-130 dropping water during training.

The Forest Service's Medium-term Approach Includes Contracting for Newer Aircraft, but Implementation Has Been Delayed

For nearly 2 years, the Forest Service has attempted to award "next-generation" contracts with durations of 5 to 10 years to modernize the fleet with faster and more up-to-date large airtankers. However, these efforts have been delayed by bid protests, and it is uncertain when some vendors will complete federal approval and certification processes for their aircraft, which are necessary prior to use as airtankers on federal contracts. As a result, it is uncertain when the "next-generation" large airtankers will be available to support fire suppression activities. Additionally, private vendors that are developing the "next-generation" large airtankers told us that concerns regarding the consistency of the Forest Service's approach to fleet modernization have increased the difficulty of making business decisions and could affect the number of aircraft they will be able to provide to the government.

In November 2011, the Forest Service issued a solicitation for "next-generation" large airtankers in an effort to modernize the airtanker fleet with more modern, capable, and safe large airtankers (see fig. 5).[54] In June 2012 the Forest Service issued an initial notice of intent to award contracts for seven aircraft. However, protests that challenged the announced awards were filed and consequently those contracts were not awarded. The Forest Service subsequently issued an amended solicitation, and in May 2013, the Forest Service announced contract awards for seven aircraft,[55] with the intent that these aircraft be available for use during the 2013 fire season. While the second round of "next-generation" large airtanker awards was also protested by a vendor, this protest was dropped in June 2013.

---

[54]The "next-generation" large airtanker contract solicitation allowed for the award of up to seven exclusive-use contracts, each with up to five aircraft, with 5-year base durations followed by five 1-year option periods to be selected at the discretion of the Forest Service. It stipulated that candidate aircraft be turbine-powered, capable of cruising at speeds of at least 300 knots, and have a retardant capacity of at least 2,400 gallons, with a target capacity of 3,000 to 5,000 gallons. The solicitation indicated that aircraft with a capacity of 3,000 gallons or more would be evaluated higher than those aircraft offered with less capacity and would be considered first when determining awards. However, several vendors questioned the rationale behind the 3,000-5,000 gallon target, telling us that the aircraft available for the large airtanker mission with retardant capacities in the 2,000 to 2,500 gallon range may be more capable, available, and less expensive to operate.

[55]Five vendors received contract awards for a total of seven aircraft. The seven aircraft were two Avro RJ85s, two McDonnell Douglas MD-87s, one BAe-146, one Lockheed Martin C-130Q, and one DC-10. All of these aircraft can carry between 3,000 and 5,000 gallons of retardant, according to Forest Service officials, with the exception of the DC-10, a very large airtanker capable of carrying 11,600 gallons. The DC-10 "next generation" contract flight hour rate includes the delivery of 5,000 gallons of retardant, although the aircraft can deliver its full capacity at a higher flight hour rate.

Figure 5: Example of a "Next-Generation" Large Airtanker (BAe-146)

Source: GAO.

Note: Minden Air Corp. owns this BAe-146 and is modifying it with the addition of a traditional gravity-fed retardant delivery system.

It is uncertain when all of the "next-generation" large airtankers will be available to support fire suppression activities because only one of these aircraft has completed necessary federal approval and certification processes. Specifically, the DC-10 very large airtanker has completed the Interagency Airtanker Board's approval process, which the Forest Service considers a prerequisite for delivering retardant in support of fire suppression activities. According to Forest Service officials, the remaining vendors originally scheduled the testing of their aircraft and retardant delivery systems for spring 2013. However, Forest Service officials also told us that, as of August 8, 2013, none of these aircraft had completed testing, which is now scheduled to continue later into the year. Additionally, they told us that only the DC-10 had received Federal Aviation Administration certification to be modified for operation as an airtanker, which is required by the Forest Service prior to aircraft delivering retardant.[56]

---

[56]Such approval is granted through a "supplemental type certificate," which is issued when a vendor has received Federal Aviation Administration approval to modify an aircraft from its original design.

Based on their experience with the Forest Service over the last several years, large airtanker vendors told us that they have a limited understanding of the agency's approach to fleet modernization. Specifically, they stated that the Forest Service has varied in the number and ownership structure (i.e., vendor, government, or a mix of the two) of large airtankers it plans to have in its fleet. As early as 2005, the Forest Service indicated it would rely on a fleet of government-owned Lockheed Martin C-130J Hercules aircraft, a substantial departure from the agency's longtime practice of relying on private vendors to supply firefighting aircraft. The 2009 *Interagency Aviation Strategy* called for a government-owned fleet of 25 new C-130Js and stated that the future federal use of privately-owned large airtankers was highly unlikely due to concerns regarding safety, cost, and aircraft availability. Yet the Forest Service's 2012 *Large Airtanker Modernization Strategy* stated that the agency will rely on private vendors to provide at least a portion of the intended large airtanker fleet, which it noted is likely between 18 and 28 aircraft.

Representatives of some large airtanker vendors we spoke with said that this inconsistency in the Forest Service's large airtanker approach has increased the difficulty of making business investment decisions. For example, some vendors told us that if they were confident that the Forest Service's long-term plans would include privately-owned large airtankers as a significant portion of its future large airtanker fleet, they might be more inclined to invest in the modification of additional aircraft. Some vendors also told us that a 10-year contract term—rather than the current practice of awarding contracts with 5-year base terms and five 1-year options—would create greater stability in the large airtanker market and could result in lower costs for the federal government by allowing vendors to recoup their aircraft investment costs over 10 years instead of 5.[57]

---

[57]The 2009 *Interagency Aviation Strategy* also identified the use of 10-year contracts as a goal for federal firefighting aircraft acquisition programs. However, Forest Service officials noted that the agency does not currently have the statutory authority to issue 10-year aviation contracts and that the 5-year duration of the "next generation" contracts is longer than the agency has typically issued.

Forest Service's Long-term Approach Includes Government-Owned Airtankers, but Concerns Exist Regarding Cost and Effectiveness

The Forest Service's 2012 Large Airtanker Modernization Strategy stated that the agency must continue to explore different acquisition models—including government-owned aircraft and vendor-owned aircraft under contract to the agency—to ensure the agency will have access to large airtankers over the long term. The strategy did not identify the agency's planned ratio of government-owned to vendor-owned aircraft, and Forest Service officials told us that such determinations have not yet been made. The strategy also did not specify the type of government-owned aircraft to be obtained, but a senior official in the Forest Service's Fire and Aviation Management program told us that the agency is planning to acquire a mix of Lockheed Martin C-130J Hercules and Alenia C-27J Spartan aircraft with expected service life spans of up to 30 years. However, potential acquisition or operational challenges are associated with both types of government-owned aircraft the Forest Service is proposing.

Lockheed Martin C-130J Hercules

While the Forest Service has indicated its long-term intention to rely on a government-owned fleet of C-130Js to meet some or all of its large airtanker needs,[58] the agency has been unable to demonstrate the feasibility of this approach to OMB, which would need to approve such an investment. The Forest Service estimates in its 2012 *Large Airtanker Modernization Strategy* that each new aircraft would cost $79 million,[59] not including costs related to operations or maintenance.[60] Since 2005, the Forest Service has submitted two proposals for the government purchase of a large airtanker fleet to OMB for review and potential inclusion in budget requests. However, OMB officials told us that the agency rejected both of these proposals because they were incomplete and did not meet agency guidance.[61] After reviewing these proposals, the Department of Agriculture's Office of Inspector General concluded in a 2009 audit report that the Forest Service needed to establish better

---

[58]The Forest Service has also indicated that these would be used as multirole aircraft capable of transporting cargo and personnel when not in use as airtankers.

[59]This represents a $19 million increase over the $60 million per-aircraft cost estimate stated in the Forest Service's large airtanker appendix to the 2009 *Interagency Aviation Strategy*.

[60]Although the Forest Service proposed the acquisition of new C-130Js, a senior official told us the agency would also accept used C-130Js if they were declared surplus by DOD.

[61]Guidance on such submissions is contained in OMB Circular A-11, "Preparation, Submission, and Execution of the Budget" (August 2012), and OMB Circular A-126, "Improving the Management and Use of Government Aircraft" (May 22, 1992).

performance measures in coordination with interagency stakeholders and collect performance data on the use and effectiveness of airtankers.[62] According to Forest Service officials, another proposal has been submitted for Department of Agriculture management review, but the department has not established a time frame for submitting the proposal to OMB. However, it is unclear whether the Forest Service has resolved the concerns of both OMB and the Inspector General. Additionally, Forest Service and Interior officials stated that the effectiveness of the C-130J will largely depend on the type of retardant delivery system installed. In particular, the officials expressed concern that equipping the aircraft with MAFFS-like units similar to those used in military C-130 aircraft—which the agency has indicated is an option—could be problematic given the previously discussed limitations of that type of retardant delivery system. In addition, obtaining such units could be problematic because there is no existing manufacturer of MAFFS units,[63] although the Forest Service issued a request for information from potential manufacturers regarding the development of new retardant delivery system designs.

Alenia C-27J Spartan

The Forest Service has also expressed interest in obtaining up to 14 Alenia C-27J Spartan transport aircraft from DOD if they are declared surplus equipment.[64] Forest Service documents indicate that the agency would benefit from acquiring these aircraft for several reasons. Specifically, agency documents cited that the C-27J aircraft would be safer and more reliable than "legacy" large airtankers, in part because they are newer and have improved structural designs; they could be used in multiple roles that include dropping retardant and carrying cargo or smokejumpers; their flight speed exceeds the 300-knot requirement under the "next-generation" contract; and the agency would not have to pay to acquire the aircraft—which officials described as a critical benefit— although it would incur costs to convert the aircraft to firefighting use.

Despite the advantages cited by the agency, several challenges may exist with operating the aircraft to support fire suppression activities,

---

[62]Department of Agriculture Office of Inspector General, *Audit Report: Forest Service's Replacement Plan for Firefighting Aerial Resources* (Washington, D.C.: July 16, 2009).

[63]The manufacturer of the MAFFS units used by DOD ceased operating in 2011.

[64]A provision in the Fiscal Year 2013 National Defense Authorization Act grants the Forest Service preference over other agencies in acquiring seven of these aircraft for use in the firefighting mission if the aircraft are declared surplus by DOD.

including some related to the aircraft's capacity and capabilities. For example, an analysis conducted by a private consultant for the Forest Service indicated that the maximum retardant capacity of the C-27J is expected to be about 1,850 gallons, which is below the minimum 2,400 gallon retardant capacity the agency established for its "next-generation" large airtanker fleet.[65] Depending on how the aircraft are used, the actual capacity may be substantially lower. Specifically, the Forest Service has indicated that it would use the C-27Js as multirole aircraft, transporting cargo and smokejumpers when they are not being used as airtankers. To do so, the agency initially stated that it expected to rely on removable, pressurized retardant delivery systems similar to MAFFS units described earlier to allow the aircraft to carry out this multirole mission.[66] However, according to the Forest Service consultant, such a system would carry about 1,100 gallons. Some agency officials told us that they are concerned about the retardant capacity of the aircraft, particularly if a removable, pressurized delivery system is used. Specifically, they questioned whether the C-27J would be able to carry enough retardant to provide a useful resource to firefighters and noted that pressurized retardant delivery systems do not always provide adequate coverage on the ground to support fire suppression operations. More recently, Forest Service officials stated that the agency expects to use a removable, gravity-fed retardant delivery system rather than a pressurized system, which would likely alleviate some concerns regarding the system's capabilities. The agency stated that it is currently examining alternatives and will make a decision regarding the delivery system at the conclusion of that analysis.

Other potential challenges relate to uncertainties about the costs of operating and maintaining the aircraft, which the Forest Service would be responsible for under the 2013 National Defense Authorization Act. For example, the consultant hired by the Forest Service to analyze the C-27Js reported that, although there is a significant advantage in having the aircraft transferred without acquisition cost, the costs to maintain and

---

[65]*C-27J Capabilities and Cost Analysis Report* (undated), submitted in October 2012 to the Forest Service by Convergent Performance, LLC.

[66]The Chief of the Forest Service, in testimony before the Senate Committee on Appropriations, Subcommittee on Interior, Environment, and Related Agencies on May 22, 2013 and the Senate Committee on Energy and Natural Resources on June 4, 2013, stated that the agency was considering equipping any C-27Js obtained with MAFFS-like retardant delivery systems.

operate these aircraft are uncertain and could present challenges. A Forest Service official told us that the agency estimates the cost to modify each aircraft for the airtanker mission would range from $1 million to $4.25 million and delivery time frames would range from 6 months to 40 months, but the actual figures depend on the type of system selected.[67] Further, DOD officials responsible for managing the C-27J told us they expect the cost to maintain the aircraft to rise at the conclusion of DOD's current contract with a private vendor and stated that the Forest Service would need to establish new maintenance and training contracts, which could be complex to manage. According to both DOD officials and the Forest Service consultant's analysis, domestic flight training for this aircraft is available from a single provider, which the consultant indicated is "time consuming...and relatively expensive." Forest Service officials stated that they have not yet been able to access detailed information on DOD's experience with C-27J operations and maintenance costs and have not obtained information from the manufacturer to fully understand and analyze the costs of operating the aircraft.

Some Federal and State Agencies Are Considering Alternatives to Relying on Federal Large Airtankers

Although the Forest Service has taken several steps to modernize the large airtanker fleet, as noted, the number of large airtankers available under federal contract decreased from 44 in 2002 to 8 in early 2013. As a result, some federal and state agencies are looking to alternative plans to suppress fires. For example, for the 2013 fire season, Interior increased the number of single-engine airtankers on exclusive-use contracts from 14 to 28 in part due to concerns about the availability of large airtankers. Interior officials noted that the use of single-engine airtankers has increased over the last decade as fewer large airtankers have been available. Interior also plans to rely on the capabilities of an additional 46 single-engine airtankers on call-when-needed contracts to provide additional support in 2013.[68] Following the termination of contracts for 8 large airtankers in 2011 due to safety concerns, the Forest Service has increased the number of large helicopters available on exclusive-use contract by 8, for a total of 34, from fiscal year 2011 to fiscal year 2012.

---

[67]A Forest Service official told us that the agency estimates that the cost to refurbish and equip the aircraft for the smokejumper and cargo missions could be up to $900,000 per aircraft.

[68]Because these aircraft are not on exclusive-use contracts, their availability is not guaranteed.

Further, some states are taking actions to enhance their own abilities to obtain their own aerial firefighting support. For example, CAL FIRE officials told us that, as the result of concerns regarding the Forest Service's ability to consistently provide a large airtanker fleet to suppress fires in California, CAL FIRE may consider expanding its firefighting aircraft fleet to include large airtankers.[69] In the wake of similar concerns about aerial firefighting support for fires such as those that caused extensive damage in 2012,[70] Colorado has enacted legislation that authorizes a firefighting aircraft fleet for its state.[71] In addition, Nebraska has enacted a bill that authorizes the state to contract for two single-engine airtankers.[72]

Conclusions

Recognizing the importance of aircraft to help fight wildland fires, the Forest Service and Interior have undertaken efforts to identify the number and type of firefighting aircraft they need over the years but have met with limited success. None of the agencies' studies and strategy documents contained information on aircraft performance and effectiveness in supporting firefighting operations, which limits the agencies' understanding of the strengths and limitations of each type of firefighting aircraft and their abilities to identify the number and type of aircraft they need. The Forest Service has started to collect some aircraft performance information, but it is limited and focused on large airtankers. Interior has no current plans to collect performance information on the aircraft it manages. Agencies have also engaged in limited collaboration with each other and with other stakeholders in the fire aviation community— including the private aircraft vendors on whom the Forest Service has traditionally relied to provide large airtankers. Incorporating input from all fire aviation community stakeholders in their strategic planning documents could better position the Forest Service and Interior in developing estimates of aircraft needs to include in their strategies that

---

[69]CAL FIRE operates and maintains 23 Grumman S-2T Tracker airtankers (former naval anti-submarine aircraft with retardant capacities of 1,200 gallons each), 16 North American-Rockwell OV-10 Bronco surveillance aircraft, and 11 Bell UH-1H Super Huey helicopters.

[70]The 2012 Waldo Canyon and High Park fires cumulatively burned a total of 105,531 acres, cost nearly $56 million to suppress, and destroyed at least 605 homes.

[71]C.R.S.A. §§ 24-33.5-1203(u); 24-33.5-1228.

[72]N.R.S. §§ 81-825 to 81-828.

represent the national need for firefighting aircraft. This concern is illustrated by the variety of federal and state agencies taking steps to compensate for the decline in large airtankers, which highlights the number of parties affected by firefighting aircraft decisions and reinforces the need for collaboration. Overall, better knowledge about aircraft effectiveness—and more complete input from all involved parties—could inform Forest Service and Interior decisions and help them ensure the adequacy of the nation's firefighting aircraft fleet. The challenges faced by the Forest Service in each phase of its large airtanker approach, which includes the potential acquisition of aircraft the federal government would own and operate for decades, underscore the need for a complete and collective understanding of the nation's firefighting aircraft needs.

Recommendations for Executive Action

To help the agencies enhance their abilities to identify their firefighting aircraft needs and better ensure they obtain aircraft that meet those needs, we recommend that the Secretaries of Agriculture and the Interior direct the Chief of the Forest Service and the Deputy Assistant Secretary for Public Safety, Resource Protection, and Emergency Services, respectively, to take the following three actions:

- Expand efforts to collect information on aircraft performance and effectiveness to include all types of firefighting aircraft in the federal fleet;
- Enhance collaboration between the agencies and with stakeholders in the fire aviation community to help ensure that agency efforts to identify the number and type of firefighting aircraft they need reflect the input of all stakeholders in the fire aviation community; and
- Subsequent to the completion of the first two recommendations, update the agencies' strategy documents for providing a national firefighting aircraft fleet to include analysis based on information on aircraft performance and effectiveness and to reflect input from stakeholders throughout the fire aviation community.

Agency Comments and Our Evaluation

We provided the Departments of Agriculture, Defense, and the Interior with a draft of this report for their review and comment.

The Forest Service (responding on behalf of the Department of Agriculture) and Interior generally agreed with our findings and recommendations, and their written comments are reproduced in appendixes IV and V respectively. The Forest Service and Interior also provided technical comments which we incorporated as appropriate. The Department of Defense did not provide comments.

While the Forest Service generally agreed with our findings and recommendations and stated that it is committed to improving its collaboration efforts, it also reiterated its interest in obtaining C-27Js to augment its aerial firefighting capabilities, citing the benefit of low initial investment for aircraft that could potentially function in multiple roles. As stated in our report, we acknowledge the Forest Service's incentive to obtain the C-27Js free of acquisition cost and their potential use in multiple roles. We also note, however, that the agency may face challenges regarding the retardant capacity and operating costs associated with the airtankers.

We are sending copies of this report to the Secretaries of Agriculture, Defense, and the Interior; the Chief of the Forest Service; the Directors of the Bureau of Indian Affairs, Bureau of Land Management, Fish and Wildlife Service, and National Park Service; appropriate congressional committees; and other interested parties. In addition, the report is available at no charge on the GAO website at http://www.gao.gov.

If you or your staff members have any questions about this report, please contact me at (202) 512-3841 or fennella@gao.gov. Contact points for our Office of Congressional Relations and Public Affairs may be found on the last page of this report. Key contributors to this report are listed in appendix VI.

Anne-Marie Fennell
Director, Natural Resources and Environment

Appendix I: Objectives, Scope, and Methodology

This report examines (1) Forest Service and Department of the Interior efforts undertaken to identify the number and type of firefighting aircraft they need and (2) the Forest Service's approach to modernizing the large airtanker fleet and the challenges it faces in doing so.

To examine Forest Service and Interior efforts to identify their firefighting aircraft needs, we reviewed major agency studies and strategy documents and interviewed agency officials responsible for managing fire aviation programs. We focused on those efforts conducted since 1995, when the Forest Service and Interior jointly conducted the first major study of their large airtanker needs. We reviewed the purpose, methodology, and results of each of these studies and strategy documents. We also reviewed seven academic and government studies on aerial firefighting and conducted interviews with agency officials, as well as officials representing stakeholders in the fire aviation community, including military, state, and international firefighting organizations, and companies that own and operate firefighting aircraft, to identify key elements that are important for understanding firefighting aircraft needs.[1] (Information on the stakeholders included in our review is discussed in more detail later in this appendix.) Through these document reviews and interviews, and in consultation with internal GAO stakeholders including methodological specialists and staff knowledgeable about aviation contracting, we identified the following key elements: aircraft types, basing options, acquisition models, aircraft capabilities, suppression methods, and aircraft performance and effectiveness. We then reviewed the agency efforts to determine the extent to which each effort included analysis of these key elements.

We also interviewed agency officials about the extent of collaboration involved in agency efforts to identify the number and type of firefighting aircraft they need. In light of the information collected, we reviewed our prior work on interagency collaboration and key practices that can help enhance and sustain collaborative efforts, and compared the practices of the formal body for coordination among aerial firefighting agencies—the National Interagency Aviation Committee—with key collaboration practices to determine the extent to which the committee's practices were

---

[1] We considered the methodologies of the academic and government studies that we reviewed and determined that the results of the studies were sufficiently reliable for the purpose of identifying key elements that are important for understanding firefighting aircraft needs.

consistent with key practices we previously identified. The key practices
we evaluated were: defining and articulating a common outcome;
establishing mutually reinforcing or joint strategies to achieve the
outcome; identifying and addressing needs by leveraging resources;
agreeing upon agency roles and responsibilities; establishing compatible
policies, procedures, and other means to operate across agency
boundaries; developing mechanisms to monitor, evaluate, and report the
results of collaborative efforts; and reinforcing agency accountability for
collaborative efforts through agency plans and reports.[2] GAO has also
identified reinforcing individual accountability for collaborative efforts
through agency performance management systems as a best practice for
coordination, but we did not consider this practice in our assessment
because performance management systems fell outside the scope of this
review.

To examine the Forest Service's approach to modernizing the large
airtanker fleet and the challenges it faces in doing so, we reviewed
agency documents related to large airtanker acquisition, management,
and operations and interviewed agency officials to identify the agency's
approach to obtaining these aircraft. We reviewed agency planning and
acquisition documents, such as the National Interagency Aviation
Committee's 2009 *Interagency Aviation Strategy*, the Forest Service's
2012 *Large Airtanker Modernization Strategy*, and Forest Service
airtanker contract solicitations, which lay out the Forest Service's
approach to obtaining large airtankers in the short, medium, and long
terms.

To collect information in support of both objectives, we interviewed
members of the fire aviation stakeholder community, including officials
involved in the management and operations of aerial firefighting from the
Forest Service, Interior and its four land management bureaus, the
Department of Defense, six state agencies that we selected based on
input from federal agencies and the National Association of State
Foresters, and the British Columbia Forest Service; representatives from
eight of the nine vendors we identified that own, operate, and maintain
large airtankers and that have responded to the most recent Forest
Service contract solicitations;[3] and two national trade organizations—one

---

[2]GAO-06-15. We identified these practices through reviewing relevant literature and
interviewing experts in the area of collaboration.

[3]Representatives of the ninth vendor did not respond to our attempts to contact them.

that represents firefighting aircraft vendors and one that represents
pilots—which we identified based on conversations with agency officials
and vendor representatives. We also conducted site visits to the National
Interagency Fire Center in Boise, Idaho; the facilities of the only two
private vendors with current Forest Service "legacy" large airtanker
contracts, located in Minden, Nevada, and Missoula, Montana; the
manufacturing facility of a company that produces single-engine
airtankers in Olney, Texas; and the headquarters of California's fire
aviation program —part of the California Department of Forestry and Fire
Protection (CAL FIRE) in Sacramento—which manages more airtankers
than the Forest Service. The results of our interviews and site visits are
not generalizable.

We conducted this performance audit from August 2012 to August 2013
in accordance with generally accepted government auditing standards.
Those standards require that we plan and perform the audit to obtain
sufficient, appropriate evidence to provide a reasonable basis for our
findings and conclusions based on our audit objectives. We believe that
the evidence obtained provides a reasonable basis for our findings and
conclusions based on our audit objectives.

The Forest Service and Interior contract for, and to a lesser extent own, a variety of aircraft used to help suppress wildland fires. Table 2 provides information, as reported by Forest Service and Interior contracting officials, on the federal firefighting aircraft fleet for the 2013 fire season, including aircraft type, number available, and cost rates.

Table 2: Type, Number, and Cost Rates for Federally-Contracted Firefighting Aircraft

Aircraft type	Exclusive-use contracts			Call-when-needed contracts		
	Number of aircraft	Daily availability rate	Flight hour rate	Number of aircraft	Daily availability rate	Flight hour rate
Very large airtanker[a,b,c]	1	$26,750	$4,553-$12,500	2	$51,522-$75,000	$7,668-$12,000
Large airtanker[a,c]	15	$10,700-$34,000	$4,400-$9,996	0	-	-
Single-engine airtanker[d,e]	28	$1,700-$4,076	$1,500-$3,988	46	$2,225-$4,150	$2,305-$4,242
Water scooper[e]	2	$9,859	$6,363-$7,918	1	$11,549	$7,158-$8,637
Large helicopter[c]	34	$9,256-$25,942	$1,958-$7,828	85	$13,320-$46,900	$2,967-$23,300
Medium helicopter[c]	33	$4,050-$11,600	$1,748-$1,998	101	$3,600-$19,815	$1,732-$2,445
Small helicopter	78	$950-$5,775	$330-$2,350	[f]	$1,000-$12,975	$325-$2,691
Forest Service	53	$950-$3,136	$860-$1,193	195	$2,044-$5,320	$836-$1,768
Interior	25	$1,750-$5,775	$330-$2,350	345	$1,000-$12,975	$325-$2,691
Surveillance aircraft[g]	50	$569-$5,861	$225-$4,934	90	$485-$3,850	$309-$2,419
Forest Service	28	$1,806-$2,254	$598	0	-	-
Interior	22	$569-$5,861	$225-$4,934	90	$485-$3,850	$309-$2,419
Smokejumper aircraft	14	$3,315-$5,597	$950-$2,020	1	$4,600	$1,300
Forest Service[h]	12	$3,330-$5,597	$950-$2,020	0	-	-
Interior	2	$3,315-$3,400	$973-$1,026	1	$4,600	$1,300

Sources: Forest Service and Interior contracting officials.

[a]Flight hour rates do not include the cost of aircraft fuel.

[b]The DC-10 available on exclusive-use was awarded a contract under the "next generation" large airtanker solicitation and has a flight hour rate of $4,553 for delivering 5,000 gallons and $12,500 for delivering 11,600 gallons of retardant.

[c]The Forest Service contracts for these aircraft.

[d]Includes one exclusive-use and three call-when needed amphibious, water-scooping single-engine airtankers.

[e]Interior contracts for these aircraft.

[f]We did not determine the total number of aircraft available because some vendors may have a single aircraft available on call-when-needed contracts with both the Forest Service and Interior.

[g]This category includes exclusive-use and call-when-needed lead planes as well as two Forest Service-owned infrared mapping aircraft; the availability costs of the infrared fire mapping aircraft are calculated on a monthly basis and range from $23,064 to $29,174.

[h]This category includes the seven smokejumper aircraft owned by the Forest Service; the availability costs of these aircraft are calculated on a monthly basis and range from $11,972 to $23,476.

Since 1995, the Forest Service and Interior have conducted or contracted for nine major studies and strategy documents that identify firefighting aircraft needs. Table 3 provides information on major efforts conducted by, or on behalf of, the Forest Service and Interior to identify the number and type of firefighting aircraft they need.

Table 3: Purpose, Methodology, and Recommendations of Major Efforts to Identify Federal Firefighting Aircraft Needs, by Date

Author(s)	Purpose	Methodology used	Number and type of aircraft recommended
1995, *National Study of Airtankers to Support Initial Attack and Large Fire Suppression: Final Report Phase 1*			
Forest Service and Interior	Provide analytical support and develop models to identify the most effective and efficient utilization of airtankers and to optimize the currently available airtanker fleet and find the best base locations	Compared the cost of the 1995 large airtanker program—41 airtankers—with a series of alternatives, including no airtanker program, a smaller airtanker program, and moving airtankers to different base locations to determine the most efficient basing of large airtankers	41 large airtankers[a,b]
1996, *National Study of (Large) Airtankers to Support Initial Attack and Large Fire Suppression: Final Report Phase 2*			
Forest Service and Interior	Provide information on reasonable airtanker base locations and airtanker fleet possibilities to guide modernization of the airtanker program	Analyzed potential airtanker types and base locations using set of evaluation criteria—compatibility with airtanker bases, initial attack efficiency, large fire support, accuracy and performance, availability, viable vendors, and reality/professional judgment check—to determine the number and size of airtankers to station at each base	41 large airtankers[a,b]
1998, *National Study of Tactical Aerial Resource Management to Support Initial Attack and Large Fire Suppression: Final Committee Report*			
Forest Service and Interior	Determine the appropriate organization, locations, and aerial platforms to safely and cost effectively manage and direct aerial fire suppression resources	Compared available surveillance aircraft against a set of evaluation criteria, such as required technology, minimum speed, and minimum personnel capacity to determine the appropriate type of surveillance aircraft, and identified the number of surveillance aircraft needed based on the number of large airtankers recommended by the 1995 and 1996 studies	41 surveillance aircraft[c]
2005, *Wildland Fire Management Aerial Application Study*			
Fire Program Solutions, LLC	For initial attack, recommend most cost efficient large aircraft type and number by base and recommend performance attributes for airtankers and large helicopters to support cost efficient national program; for large fire support, determine airtanker and helicopter requirements	Analyzed the most efficient locations to place airtankers, by geographic area, and identified the scenario with the lowest total fire suppression, airtanker program, and potential fire damage costs; identified the most efficient combination of exclusive-use and call-when-needed large helicopters based on demand and cost	34-41 large airtankers[b]

Author(s)	Purpose	Methodology used	Number and type of aircraft recommended
2008, _Management Efficiency Assessment on Aviation Activities in the USDA Forest Service_			
Management Analysis, Incorporated	Identify areas within the Forest Service aviation activities that can be improved through efficiencies in staffing, organization, communications, technology, and procedures	Compared the "as-is" conditions with desired "to-be" conditions for six Forest Service areas— aerial delivery of firefighters; aerial detection and command and control; aerial fire suppression—airtanker and large helicopter; aerial resources support; aviation contract management and quality assurance; and aviation program management—and conducted a cost/benefit analysis to identify recommendations for improving efficiency within each area	19 large airtankers[b]
2009, _National Interagency Aviation Council Interagency Aviation Strategy_			
Forest Service, Bureau of Indian Affairs, Bureau of Land Management, Interior, Fish and Wildlife Service, National Park Service, and National Association of State Foresters	Develop an aviation strategy for federal wildland fire agencies, including strategies for the organization, procurement, and management of aviation resources used in federal wildland firefighting	Identified the number of each type of aircraft needed in the national firefighting aircraft fleet by using numbers from preceding aviation program studies, simple demand analysis, and current program aircraft totals	32 large airtankers 3 water scoopers 35 single-engine airtankers 45 surveillance aircraft 19 smokejumper aircraft 34 large helicopters 47 medium helicopters 100 small helicopters
2012, _Forest Service Large Airtanker Modernization Strategy_			
Forest Service	Document the strategy for ensuring that the nation is equipped with a viable fleet of large airtankers	Analyzed options for large airtankers, based on the large airtanker requirements identified in the 1996 National Study of (Large) Airtankers to Support Initial Attack and Large Fire Suppression, Phase 2 and the 2009 National Interagency Aviation Council Interagency Aviation Strategy	18-28 large airtankers[b]
2012, _Air Attack Against Wildfires: Understanding U.S. Forest Service Requirements for Large Aircraft_			
Rand Corporation	Determined the composition of a fleet of large airtankers, water scooping aircraft, and large helicopters that would minimize the total costs of wildfires, including the cost of large fires and the cost of aircraft	Analyzed various compositions of a fleet of large airtankers, water scooping aircraft, and large helicopters to determine which composition would minimize the total costs of wildfires, including federal, state, and local suppression costs; post-fire rehabilitation costs; insured losses; fatalities; future suppression costs; and the cost of the prospective aircraft	1-9 large airtankers[d] 14-55 water scoopers 0-7 large helicopters

Author(s)	Purpose	Methodology used	Number and type of aircraft recommended
2013, *Firefighting Aircraft Study*			
Avid LLC	Develop a performance measure that directly demonstrated cost-impact of large airtankers and heavy helicopters in firefighting	Used a supply and demand model to determine the annual number of airtanker orders that the Forest Service has been unable to fill with its contracted large airtankers	35 large airtankers are needed to fill 90 percent of requests for large airtankers[e]

Source: GAO analysis.

[a]This total of 41 includes 30 airtankers contracted by the Forest Service, 6 airtankers contracted by Interior, and 5 airtankers contracted by states.

[b]This study recommended the appropriate number of large airtankers and did not recommend an appropriate number of other types of firefighting aircraft.

[c]This study recommended the appropriate number of aerial surveillance aircraft and did not recommend an appropriate number of other types of firefighting aircraft.

[d]This study focused on the Forest Service's large airtankers, water scoopers, and large helicopters, and did not recommend an appropriate number for other types of firefighting aircraft.

[e]This study focused on the Forest Service's large airtankers and large helicopters and did not recommend an appropriate number of large helicopters.

Appendix IV: Comments from the Department of Agriculture

USDA	United States Department of Agriculture	Forest Service	Washington Office	1400 Independence Avenue, SW Washington, DC 20250

File Code: 1420

Date: AUG 0 6 2013

Ms. Anne-Marie Fennell
Director, Natural Resources and Environment
U.S. Government Accountability Office
441 G. Street, N.W.
Washington, DC 20548

Dear Ms. Fennell:

Thank you for the opportunity to review and comment on the draft U.S. Government Accountability Office (GAO) Report on "Wildland Fire Management: Improvements Needed in Information, Collaboration, and Planning to Enhance Federal Fire Aviation Program Success" (GAO-13-684). The Forest Service has reviewed the draft report and generally agrees with its findings and recommendations, with some concerns as noted. Technical comments are attached.

The Forest Service works with its partners and stakeholders on all aspects of the fire management program, and aviation is no exception. To develop the 2012 Large Airtanker Modernization Strategy (Strategy), we took information gathered from the National Interagency Aviation Committee (NIAC) and worked with the Department of the Interior's Office of Wildland Fire to tailor the Strategy for both Departments' needs. The awarding of contracts for seven next generation large airtankers is a significant step forward towards implementing the Strategy. We know we have more work to do on collaboration, and we plan to do so. The Strategy will be updated to reflect this work, and will include the results of the information we are collecting on aircraft effectiveness.

Although it was not identified in earlier documentation, such as the Strategy, the Forest Service believes that the C-27J can fill a niche in the aerial firefighting system. The availability of a medium-sized aircraft, for little investment, provides the Forest Service with great capability. Even though this medium airtanker requirement was not previously identified, it is a very opportune capability that comes with the DOD divestiture of the C-27J, and offers extra surge capacity in addition to Modular Airborne Firefighting System (MAFFS). The C-27J will allow the Forest Service to augment the large airtanker fleet with a capable medium airtanker as well as modernize the smokejumper fleet and perform team and cargo transport. Operational plans are developed as part of the process of transitioning new aircraft into the agency. That will be the case with the C-27J, and is expected to be very similar to the operational plan now in use by the comparable size P-2V airtanker (1,800 gal vs. 2,000 gal).

The Forest Service is committed to working with its partners and stakeholders to improve coordination and collaboration related to fire and aviation programs, including aviation. We are committed to improving our efforts and coordination with the Department of the Interior and our other partners and stakeholders.

Caring for the Land and Serving People

Printed on Recycled Paper

2

Ms. Anne-Marie Fennell, Director of Natural Resource Environment, U.S. Government
Accountability Office

Thank you again for the opportunity to review your draft report. If you have any questions,
please contact Thelma Strong, Chief Financial Officer, at 202-205-1321 or tstrong@fs.fed.us.
Sincerely,

Thomas L. Tidwell

THOMAS L. TIDWELL
Chief

Appendix V: Comments from the Department of the Interior

United States Department of the Interior

OFFICE OF THE SECRETARY
Washington, D.C. 20240

AUG 8 2013

Ms. Anne-Marie Fennell
Director, Natural Resources and Environment
U.S. Government Accountability Office
441 G Street, N.W.
Washington, D.C. 20548

Dear Ms. Fennell:

Thank you for providing the Department of the Interior the opportunity to review and comment on the draft Government Accountability Office Report entitled *WILDLAND FIRE MANAGEMENT: Improvements Needed in Information, Collaboration, and Planning to Enhance Federal Fire Aviation Program Success* (GAO-13-684).

The Department appreciates the work of the team that prepared the report and the amount of data collected. This report is an informative summation of the complex problems associated with Wildland Fire Management aviation. Interior concurs with the findings and recommendations included in the report. In collaboration with the Forest Service we will identify appropriate corrective actions.

Enclosed for consideration as the final report is prepared are Interior's general and technical comments. If you have any questions, or need additional information, contact Jim Douglas at 202-208-7754 or Mark Bathrick at 208-433-5001.

Sincerely,

Rhea Suh
Assistant Secretary
Policy, Management and Budget

Enclosure

Appendix VI: GAO Contact and Staff Acknowledgments

GAO Contact

Anne-Marie Fennell, (202) 512-3841 or fennella@gao.gov

Staff Acknowledgments

In addition to the individual named above, Steve Gaty, Assistant Director; Kristin Hughes; Richard P. Johnson; and Matthew Tabbert made significant contributions to this report. Cheryl Arvidson, Steven Putansu, and Kiki Theodoropoulos provided technical assistance.

GAO's Mission	The Government Accountability Office, the audit, evaluation, and investigative arm of Congress, exists to support Congress in meeting its constitutional responsibilities and to help improve the performance and accountability of the federal government for the American people. GAO examines the use of public funds; evaluates federal programs and policies; and provides analyses, recommendations, and other assistance to help Congress make informed oversight, policy, and funding decisions. GAO's commitment to good government is reflected in its core values of accountability, integrity, and reliability.
Obtaining Copies of GAO Reports and Testimony	The fastest and easiest way to obtain copies of GAO documents at no cost is through GAO's website (http://www.gao.gov). Each weekday afternoon, GAO posts on its website newly released reports, testimony, and correspondence. To have GAO e-mail you a list of newly posted products, go to http://www.gao.gov and select "E-mail Updates."
Order by Phone	The price of each GAO publication reflects GAO's actual cost of production and distribution and depends on the number of pages in the publication and whether the publication is printed in color or black and white. Pricing and ordering information is posted on GAO's website, http://www.gao.gov/ordering.htm. Place orders by calling (202) 512-6000, toll free (866) 801-7077, or TDD (202) 512-2537. Orders may be paid for using American Express, Discover Card, MasterCard, Visa, check, or money order. Call for additional information.
Connect with GAO	Connect with GAO on Facebook, Flickr, Twitter, and YouTube. Subscribe to our RSS Feeds or E-mail Updates. Listen to our Podcasts. Visit GAO on the web at www.gao.gov.
To Report Fraud, Waste, and Abuse in Federal Programs	Contact: Website: http://www.gao.gov/fraudnet/fraudnet.htm E-mail: fraudnet@gao.gov Automated answering system: (800) 424-5454 or (202) 512-7470
Congressional Relations	Katherine Siggerud, Managing Director, siggerudk@gao.gov, (202) 512-4400, U.S. Government Accountability Office, 441 G Street NW, Room 7125, Washington, DC 20548
Public Affairs	Chuck Young, Managing Director, youngc1@gao.gov, (202) 512-4800 U.S. Government Accountability Office, 441 G Street NW, Room 7149 Washington, DC 20548

Please Print on Recycled Paper.

www.ingramcontent.com/pod-product-compliance
Lightning Source LLC
Chambersburg PA
CBHW080609290526
45790CB00007B/2694